P9-DED-023

Goals

Goals

PAUL H. DUNN
RICHARD M. EYRE

BOOKCRAFT, INC.
Salt Lake City, Utah

Copyright © 1976 by Bookcraft, Inc.

All rights reserved. This book or any part thereof may not be reproduced in any form whatsoever, whether by graphic, visual, electronic, filming, microfilming, tape recording or any other means, without the prior written permission of Bookcraft, Inc., except in the case of brief passages embodied in critical reviews and articles.

Library of Congress Catalog Card Number: 76-42001
ISBN 0-88494-310-0

First Printing, 1976

Lithographed in the United States of America
PUBLISHERS PRESS
Salt Lake City, Utah

Preface

All through the ages, the Lord has challenged people everywhere with an eternal goal: "Be ye therefore perfect, even as your Father which is in heaven is perfect." This challenge would not have been uttered if the attainment had not been possible. The fact is that you, yourself, have possibly reached perfection in some areas; and while total perfection may not be achieved in this life, it is ultimately possible. An anonymous writer once wrote: "Some people reach the top rung of the ladder only to find it has been leaning against the wrong wall." The gospel helps us to put the ladder against the right wall.

The format of this book is unique. We have used a sailing analogy to state the principle of how to set goals. The sailing part appears on the left-hand pages and directly parallels the goals and how to achieve them, which appear on the corresponding right-hand pages.

The table of contents is in "steps" rather than chapters and has an "S" (sailing) step for each of the seven "G" (goals) steps: e.g., Step 1, Understanding Sailing/Understanding Goal-Setting. The pages are numbered S-1, etc., and G-1, etc. S-1 and G-1 are to be read together.

We pray that you will have happy sailing as you achieve your eternal goals.

Paul H. Dunn

Richard M. Eyre

Acknowledgments

I express my gratitude to the Lord for the eternal goals he has set before me; to my wife and children for their creation of my desire to fulfill these eternal goals; to my mother and father for making the upward reach seem possible even now; to Richard Eyre, whose interest and enthusiasm makes goal-achievement exciting; and to my many friends and associates who have made the upward climb happy and pleasant.

I express further acknowledgment and appreciation to Bookcraft for their professional help. A special thanks goes to Sharene Miner for her secretarial assistance.

Paul H. Dunn

I express my appreciation for my wife and children, who are the motivation for all my goals; to Elder Paul Dunn, whose friendship has always inspired lofty goals; and to all members of this last dispensation who realize that, because of the time in which they live and the circumstances into which they were born, they cannot accept mediocrity but must reach for their stewardship and foreordination through masterful use of goals.

Richard M. Eyre

Contents

Step 1
Understanding Sailing

Step 1
Understanding Goal-Setting

As I grew up I had two friends who were also close friends
to each other.
One of them was exceptionally gifted —
tall, handsome, athletic,
an IQ close to the "genius" category;
from a wealthy family.
The other was average, toward the middle in his abilities.
As we grew older, I watched the two go different directions.
One excelled at literally everything he attempted.
Today he is the exceptional father of a fine family,
a success in business and financial affairs,
a trusted leader in church and community.
The other friend drifted, was content to just get by,
settled for a life of mediocrity and frequent frustration.

The remarkable thing is that the successful man today
was my average friend.
The mediocre, frustrated man was my gifted friend.

The thing that made my ordinary friend
extraordinary
was his well-thought goals
and his planning and tenacity in pursuing those goals.
The second friend lacked this ability, and his gifts were wasted.
The common element in all successful people
is not their looks, their intelligence, their wealth.
It is their ability to set and achieve goals.

The first requirement for successful sailing
is an understanding
of the principles that govern wind-driven vessels.
Sailboats are propelled by the force of the air against the sails
and the water against the rudder and center board.

A well-handled sailboat is so versatile
that it can sail *into* the wind
as well as with it.

Basically, there are five elements that come into play
in the process of sailing:
1. The *destination,* the place you are sailing to.
2. The *sails,* which catch and harness the wind's force.
3. The *wind* itself.
4. The *center board,* which keeps the boat from blowing sideways.
5. The *steering rudder,*
   which keeps the craft pointed toward the destination.

The first requirement for the effective use of goals
is an understanding
of what goals are and how they work.
In a sense, the mind and the nervous system
perform like a computer,
pursuing and accomplishing what they are *prepared* to do.

Properly set goals are so powerful that they can propel a person
in a direction that is contrary and even opposite
to the prevailing directions of the world around him.

Essentially there are five elements that come into play
in the goal-accomplishing process:
1. The *goal* itself, the particular thing you are trying to achieve.
2. The *plans* you formulate to guide your efforts toward the goal.
3. The *work* you put forth.
4. The *discipline* you exercise to keep moving forward
   rather than sideways.
5. The *prayers* you offer and the guidance they bring
   to stay pointed toward the goal.

To one who does not understand
the principles and techniques and forces involved,
sailing can be a dangerous business.
The sea can be a fierce and relentless enemy
with currents and undertows so strong that
a boat, once it is sucked in, cannot get out.

One great danger is for the sailor
whose destination is not entirely clear,
whose course is not adequately charted.
If indeed he gets anywhere,
he may find he has arrived at the wrong place.

Another danger is for the sailor who knows where he is bound
but lacks the complete knowledge of how to sail.
At worst he will be shipwrecked;
at best he will be frustrated as he drifts aimlessly,
unable to find the port for which he is bound.

To one who lacks comprehension
of the principles and techniques and forces involved,
goal-setting can be a dangerous business.
The world we live in is filled with the faces
of the adversary; and
if a person allows himself to be sucked into one of the
powerful currents of Satan's evil,
he may never be able to pull himself clear.

One great danger exists for the man
who either has no long-range goal or who is basically
uncertain about the purpose of mortal life.
Without any sure knowledge of long-term purpose,
he is unsure of the correctness of short-term goals,
so that if he achieves at all in life
he is uncertain whether he is achieving the right things.

Another danger is for the man who knows life's purpose
but does not know how to effectively
set and accomplish goals.
At worst he will lose sight of his purpose and ruin his life;
at best he will know the frustration
of seeing the goal but not knowing
how to get there.

(continued)

It has been said that
"the world turns aside for the man
who knows where he is going."
The tragedy is — few do.
I am reminded of a visitor to my office,
a young man in his early thirties.
He wanted to be a success in life,
to be a good husband and father,
but he had seemed to encounter failure at every turn.
I questioned him:
"What are some of your personal goals?"
"What goals do you and your wife have together?"
"What goals do you have as a family?"
His answer to all of these questions was revealing.
He hadn't given it any thought.

The Prophet Joseph Smith taught that
"the nearer a man approaches perfection,
the clearer are his views, and the greater his enjoyments,
till he has overcome the evils of his life
and lost every desire for sin. . . ."

Try the following:
1. What are five of your most important goals for your lifetime?
2. What are five of your most important goals
    for the next year of your life?
3. What would be five of your most important goals
    if you had only six months to live?
4. What have you done in the last week or intend to do
    to bring the above goals to pass?

Step 2
Knowing Your Ship and Your Sea

In addition
to understanding the general principle of sailing,
a good sailor must know his own unique boat
and the particular waters in which he sails.

Step 2
Knowing Yourself and Your World

Every child of God is unique,
both *internally* (the type of person he is, his gifts,
his limitations, his physical, mental and emotional makeup)
and *externally* (his circumstances, the part of the
world and the times and conditions in which he lives).

Therefore, a grasp of the general principles of goal-setting
is not enough.

Before meaningful goals can be set,
a person must comprehend who he truly (and uniquely) is
and what his place in eternity really consists of.

S-5

To sail safely and well, to reach his destination,
a good sailor
reads and analyzes the *external* factors that affect him:

The season of the year.

The signs and markers and buoys.

The number and type of other boats in the waters.

The weather conditions that are expected.

The currents and tides.

The position and coordinates of the destination.

For most who read this book,
the external aspects possess large fields of similarity:

We know that we are in the last days,
that our mortal lives are occurring shortly prior to the end
of this telestial earth and shortly prior to
the second coming of the Savior.

We know that we live in the dispensation of the fulness of times,
when all of the priesthood keys and gospel knowledge
ever given to men on earth
which are essential for their eternal salvation
have been restored.

Our knowledge and insight puts us in a unique position
in this unique time.
Each of us is one in one thousand
(the Church's four million in the world's four billion).

We know, because of these circumstances,
that much is expected of each of us.
(The Lord could not be pleased with an ordinary performance
by one in such extraordinary circumstances.)

We know that the world around us
is a stage for expanding wickedness;
that the pattern of compromise and immorality
parallels the patterns
that brought the downfall of other civilizations.

(continued)

G-5 (continued)

We know that our challenge, within this world,
is to return ourselves, our families and our neighbors
to the celestial kingdom
and the presence of God.

S-6

These external factors are important, demanding.
They allow no complacency
but they are, at least, rather easy to read,
and they are the same for all who sail
in these particular waters.

Beyond these generally applicable conditions
are the factors that face one sailor and one alone —
the rocks and reefs directly underneath,
the level of the tide as he approaches or departs,
and perhaps most importantly
the momentary force and direction of the wind.

These external factors are frightening, demanding.
They allow no one a feeling of complacency
but they are, at least, rather easy to read, rather clear to interpret.
Prophets have, in fact, revealed them to us;
and then, truth is uniformly applicable to all Church members
of this dispensation.

There are other external factors that
are totally un-uniform,
completely individual:
where we live, our family, our means,
the natural challenges that are set before us,
and perhaps most important of all, our opportunities,
the chances we have to contribute, to do good,
to make large or small changes in the state of our world.

S-7

It might seem that *internal* things
(about the ship itself)
would be easier to know than *external* factors.
Not so.
Weather bureaus and map-makers help the sailor
with the external;
but he knows his own craft only
through his own effort.

And unless he knows his boat —
its capacities, its limitations,
its strengths and its weaknesses —
he can never choose a destination
for which he is sure he is equipped.

At first brush, it might seem that *internal* factors
would be easier to read and interpret than *external* factors.
Not so.
To know the times and circumstances of our mortal probation
we have the help of revelation, of prophets past and present;
but to know *ourselves*
(our gifts, our stewardships, our foreordinations,
our particular purpose)
we have only the source of personal inspiration,
which is considerably harder to obtain.

Despite the difficulty,
it is clear that to set goals without knowledge of self
is an exercise in futility
(like having an unopened toolbox
and choosing a task to do
without any knowledge of what tools are in the box).

There are many ways to know a boat,
the best of which is to *live* with the craft,
to experience what it can do.

Beyond that, a sailor can do three things:
1. *Inspect*
   He can check his sheets and lines;
   he can stretch and test his sails;
   he can know if the boat's attributes are
   speed or stability, size or maneuverability,
   lightness or strength.
2. *Know the* "*specs*"
   A good sailor memorizes the "specifications" or characteristics.
   He knows how many knots his hull can endure,
   how much angle on the mast,
   how many degrees in the turn.
3. *Ask*
   A good sailor knows there are better sailors.
   He can ask.
   He can learn by listening to others who may know
   more about his boat than he does.
   He may even ask the boat's maker.

There are three basic ways of *looking for yourself*
(of discovering the *internal* factors):

1. *Analyze*
   and bring to consciousness what you already know.
   What are your natural gifts? What do you do well?
   What do you enjoy? How are you able to help other people?
   What insights, what flashes have you ever had regarding
   who you really are and what you should do with your life?

2. *Know your Patriarchal Blessing*
   Read it, read it — in fact memorize it;
   because there is no other written page
   with more meaning for you,
   and you will find things in it (single words, slight inferences)
   by memorizing it
   that you will never notice otherwise.
   A patriarchal blessing is personal revelation.
   If you read it, you'll know *about* yourself.
   If the Spirit reads it to you, you'll *know* yourself.

I know a man who has made all of his major decisions
on the basis of his patriarchal blessing.
His patriarchal blessing speaks of many blessings
in an eternal sense, some of which
will not be realized only in mortality.
These he has classified as
"eternal ends."

(continued)

He then has made specific decisions
such as a mission, marriage to his companion,
his field of study and eventual career,
on the basis of whether these would be
"means" to his "eternal ends."
He has sought divine confirmation
in each decision.
"A patriarchal blessing,"
he has indicated,
"is one of the surest guides to our happiness
when it is used."

3. Ask
   One of the most powerful admonitions in scripture is
   "ask"; and the promise is straightforward: "You will receive."
   What good father, asked by his child for bread,
   would give a stone?
   One who truly wants to know who he is,
   what he should do, one who really asks,
   will be answered
   (though it may come as the dew,
   distilling, drop by drop, from heaven).

One well-remembered day several years ago
I stood knee-deep in the Virgin River
and looked up in awe
at the thousand-foot rock cliffs of Zion's Park
on either side. The park service brochure said that the rocks
were more than 200 million years old.
I remember comparing my age to the age of the rocks
and feeling young, very young, very unimportant.

(continued)

It got dark early in the narrow canyon,
and by late afternoon I could see stars
in the narrow slice of sky above.
I recalled reading that scientists had discovered
7×10^{13} stars. (The article went on to dramatize
the magnitude of that number by saying that if there were
7×10^{13} playing cards pressed together face to face,
the line would go around the world six hundred times.)
I thought to myself:
"I am one tiny speck on one tiny world
that's going around one of those 7×10^{13} stars.
How small and totally insignificant I am."

That night, as I unrolled my sleeping bag,
a thought came to me with great impact:
"I am older than the rocks
(for my spirit is eternal).
I am more important than all 7×10^{13} stars
(because I am God's son, and they are only his handiwork)."

Step 3
Final Destination

The most obvious requirement for a successful
sailing voyage
is a destination.

A good sailor must be *sure* of his destination —
precisely where it is and what it takes to reach it.

If there is any error in his final destination,
every intermediate destination
will, by definition,
also be in error.

Step 3
Lifetime Goals

There are numerous diverse opinions
and contrasting approaches
in the scores of books
that have been written on achievement and goal-setting,
but one point on which they all agree
is the need to begin with the *long-term* and work back
to the intermediate and then the short-range.
(No one can intelligently decide which plateau to go for
this morning
until he knows which mountaintop he is trying to reach
by tonight.)

A long-term goal provides the framework
in which shorter-term goals and accompanying plans
are constructed.

One who has the wrong long-term goal
may pursue with brilliance and success the corresponding
shorter-range goals
only to find them, in the end, to be without any real
worth or value.

S-10

Clearly, a sailor who has
a marine chart
an oceanographic map on which his objective appears,
has an incalculable advantage
over a sailor with no such documents.

The sailor who sees his destination on his chart
can plot a course that leads to it.
(He can be particularly adept at this if he knows he is
returning
to a place where he has previously been.)

With that thought in mind,
it is astounding to realize that only those who have
the restored gospel
know what the long-range goal is!

To one who has the gospel, the specific lifetime goal of
"returning to the presence of God,
obtaining, with my family, the celestial kingdom"
is natural, well known, so accepted and oft-repeated
that it nearly loses its impact.

To one without the knowledge of the plan of salvation
such a goal would be revolutionary,
drastically more specific than prior vague generalities,
capable of totally changing his life
if he believed it.
Theoretically, anyone who has the long-range goal
(and who understands what is required to achieve it)
should be able to design shorter-range goals and plans
to lead himself to it.

What an incomprehensible blessing it is
to know the lifetime goal!

The sailor who knows his destination
can base upon it every decision and action —
The set of the sail, the tilt of the rudder,
the port for each night's docking.

One great wonder of sailing
is the boat's ability to move in a direction
opposite to that of the wind.
By tacking (zig-zagging)
a good sailor can pilot his craft in whatever direction
he chooses.

In one beautiful passage of scripture, the Lord tells us
his goal:
"To bring to pass the immortality and eternal life of man."
Our lifetime goal is to share his goal,
to bring about the immortality and eternal lives of
ourselves, our families, our neighbors.

That seems a simple thought,
yet if it is comprehended and believed, it influences
every decision, every action, every thought.
(Would a man who *truly* realized that
his family was the highest priority
make a decision that would adversely affect that family?)
(Would a missionary who *truly* knew the joy of
bringing salvation to others
ever engage in thoughts and actions that eroded his effectiveness?)
(Would any person *truly* knowing the eternal rewards,
forfeit them for the temporary pleasures of the world?)

Men achieve what they truly want. The saying
"Beware of what you want, for you will get it" is, over time,
inevitably true.
Thus there are no excuses. A righteous person can
move in precisely opposite directions
from those of the wicked society in which he lives.
He can, that is, if those are the goals
he chooses.

(continued)

To those who wonder (and in wondering sometimes wander)
if it is possible to live amidst wickedness
and still maintain one's goals
for a mission and temple marriage,
consider this testimony.

There are men in the Church who desired
to serve missions and marry in the temple
who, because of wartime conditions,
had to temporarily postpone those goals.
Military service is always a time
of great temptation and exposure to evil —
a time when crucial decisions are often made.
But because of goals —
a desire to come home clean;
a desire to be able to account before God
that theirs had been a life of worthiness;
a desire to marry in the house of the Lord —
it is possible, with the Lord's strength and guidance,
for LDS servicemen to withstand
the temptations and evils which parade before them.
I know this because
I was one of those servicemen.

Step 4
Intermediate Stops

Often, on a long sailing voyage,
it is the daily destination goals that are important.
Since the weather is impossible to predict
very far in advance, the success of the journey
is largely based on the new objectives set for each day.

Step 4
Intermediate Goals

It is appropriate that this chapter
is the middle step of this book,
because intermediate goals are the center, the heart,
of the goal-setting process.

Our longer-range goals are basically *given* to us by the gospel,
and our shorter-term objectives and plans
flow directly out of the intermediate.
So it is these "mid-goals" that require the greatest thought,
the clearest guidance, the brightest creativity.

It is in this setting of these "mid-goals"
that a person has to creatively *mix*
what he knows about himself, his destiny, his foreordination
with
what he knows to be his lifetime goals
and come up with specific, individual, personal
intermediate-range goals.

S-13

The more a sailor knows about his final destination
and about the sea that lies between him and it,
the more options and alternatives he will have
in setting intermediate stops
and in taking the course most acceptable in terms of
the winds and conditions of each day.

The topic of foreordination enters strongly at this point.
The Lord, through ancient and modern prophets,
has told us that we were foreordained, in the preexistence,
to certain missions on this earth.
The specificity of those foreordinations has not been revealed,
but I believe that hands were laid on our heads
and our gifts (obtained through the eternity of preexistence)
were enumerated to us; and that we were ordained
to pursue and fulfill certain purposes
consistent with those gifts and with the Lord's program
for this earth.

The great key, then,
to personal, individual goal-setting, is to know as much
as possible
about the foreordinations which the veil blocks from
our mortal minds.

The Holy Ghost has, as one of *his* missions
the task of revealing, to us,
our missions.

S-14

As much as the sailor would like to
plot his entire course at the beginning of the journey,
he generally cannot see or predict far enough ahead
to do so.
So he takes his journey a piece at a time,
with confidence that, when he arrives at one intermediate stop,
he will then be able to determine the best and safest way
to the next.

If that is the case, then, if the Holy Ghost knows
our foreordination, and if we ask the Lord to reveal it to us,
through the Holy Ghost,
should we not be able to expect a comprehensive answer,
a blueprint of our lives, on how to apply our
gifts and efforts to the precise lifetime mission
the Lord has foreordained us to?

No,
for though the Lord does reveal to some their life's mission,
their whole foreordination,
he treats most of us much differently,
helping us to build faith by opening to us the right direction
for only the next portion of our lives.

A mental picture of an incident can clarify this thought:
The locomotive engineer was asked how he could pilot his train
at eighty miles per hour, at night, when his light
allowed him to see only two hundred yards ahead.
He answered that he knew that when he had covered
that two hundred yards,
he would be able to see the next two hundred.

When going through dangerous waters,
the sailor must plot his course with extreme caution by:
1. Evaluating all alternative routes.
2. Narrowing the options by applying the criteria
    of what his boat and equipment will allow.
3. Making his best decision.
4. Confirming its correctness by checking with
    someone who has traveled that way before.

Once a person has climbed steps 1, 2, and 3
(understanding goals, knowing self, accepting the Lord's
lifetime goal)
Step 4 usually comes in two forms. First there is the question
of *what* "mid-goals" to achieve,
and then the question of in what *way* they will be achieved.
Example:
What: to graduate from college in pre-medicine,
What way: with a 3.7 grade-point average.
For the young person the "what" question may be
what to major in,
where to live,
what job to take.
For someone older, more established in a pattern,
it may be the question of how to *break* that pattern,
what new things to try to achieve or accomplish.

Whatever the age, whatever the nature of the decision,
the "setting" process should have four phases
(each phase involving thought and prayer,
both of which are aided by fasting):
1. Analyze the alternatives (starting with the broadest range
    that your lifetime goal and your knowledge of self will allow).
2. Narrow the list (by evaluating each alternative
    against the criteria of life's purpose and your personal gifts).
3. Make the best decision you can.
4. Take that decision to the Lord and ask for a
    confirmation of its correctness. (You will then receive
    either the affirmation or a stupor of thought, as
    described in Doctrine and Covenants section 9.)

S-16

The captain of a sailboat on a long journey
thinks as far ahead as weather predictability will allow.

Once the "what" question is answered,
the "way" question comes into focus.
The more specific and measurable a mid-goal is, the better.
The freshman with the goal
"to do well in college and graduate"
has nowhere near the goal-power of his companion whose goal is
"to achieve at least a 3.8 grade-point average in a
graduate school of my choice."

Usually, the longest intermediate goal should be five years or less.
(A longer goal is so far out that it fades from focus
and lacks the feel of reality.)
Out of the five-year goals grow one-year goals
which, in turn, produce monthly, then weekly objectives.

Ideally, a person should set five-year goals every year
(not every five years.)
Thus, at the end of a year, rather than being left
with a four-year goal, he redrafts and extends his vision
to produce a new set of five-year objectives
(and reaps the benefits of consistent reassessment
and of always thinking five years ahead.)

S-17

The intermediate stops on the journey
are written down — plotted on a chart in such a way
that their collective achievement
brings the boat to its final destination.

Five-year goals should be set in at least three broad areas:
The family (the well-being of your home, your spouse, your children)
The Church (callings, assignments, spiritual growth,
relationships with the Lord)
The world (school, job, community, etc.)

The one-year goals are the bricks or blocks
which, when stacked in fives, reach the five-year goals.

Sundays are ideal days for positive reflection;
for seeking personal inspiration;
in short, for goal-setting.
Each Sunday, set weekly goals (flowing from the monthly).
On fast Sundays, set monthly goals (flowing from the yearly).
On the first Sunday of the new year, set yearly goals
(flowing from five-year goals).

Write them down.
Make them specific.
Make them nest snugly into each other so that
achievement of all weekly goals
ensures the monthly, and in turn the yearly and the five-year.

Involving the Lord in the decision is important
at any appropriate stage
either of goal-setting or goal-achievement.
Learning the way to do this is vital.
Here is a personal example.

(continued)

Two years following my mission, I fell in love.
As I pondered the decision of marriage,
its eternal magnitude and consequences frightened me so badly
that I began to feel completely incapable
of ever attempting such a decision, and I concluded
that it had to be God's decision and not mine.
This seemed to me to be a very righteous attitude
and I fasted and prayed and pleaded with the Lord
to give me an answer.
But nothing came.
I recalled then the invitation of a Church leader,
Whom I had come to know on my mission,
the invitation to come to him if I needed help.

I went to his office and he graciously gave me his time.
At first he asked me questions I had already asked myself,
and I began to wonder if he could really help.
Finally he said (as if he could see my immediate past),
"You have been trying to follow Doctrine and Covenants section 9
in this decision, haven't you?"
"Yes, I have," I said, "and that is what troubles me.
I have studied it out in my mind
and I have asked the Lord for an answer,
but none has come to me."

(continued)

I remember that his eyes lit up at this point
and he smiled (having discovered the answer I needed).
"You have misunderstood the scripture," he said.
"You have left out the middle step.
You must prayerfully study it out,
then you must make your own best decision,
and then take that decision to the Lord for confirmation.
The Lord wants you to learn how to decide.
I promise you that if you will follow these steps
you will have a spiritual experience
and the Lord will confirm the correctness of your decision."

I did, and He did.

Step 5
Setting the Sails

Ponder the phrase
"setting the sails."
It means more than the simple raising of the canvas.
It implies *fixing* the right sails in the right sequence
at the right angles
(in harmony with the conditions of weather and sea
and with the force and direction of the wind)
to get the craft to the destination.

The sails are the *means*
by which the boat reaches its destination.
The sails are the *method*
by which the wind's power is harnessed and put to use.

Step 5
Setting the Plans

Ponder the phrase
"setting the plans."
It means more than the simple organizing of time.
It implies doing the right things at the right time
in the particular way
(in harmony with one's gifts and circumstances)
that allows a person to reach his goals.

Plans are the *means*
by which he reaches his goals.
Plans are the *methods*
by which a person's work and effort are harnessed
and put to effective use.

The planning function deals essentially with the
"when" and the "how"
(the "what" is answered by the yearly,
monthly and weekly goals).
The "when" question is one of time allotment
(how much time it will take and when that time
will be used).
The "how" question is the tougher one, and the one
requiring (or allowing) the greater degree of creativity.

The type of sail required depends on the wind conditions
and on the distance of the destination.
Strong, erratic wind may dictate the smallest jib sail,
while a steady predictable leeward breeze
and a distant destination
calls for the largest billowing spinnaker.

The amount and depth of "how" planning
depends on the nature of the goal.
Some goals virtually dictate the "how,"
while others require research and strong creative effort.
In either case, however, the "how" comes before the "when."

A student with the goal of an "A" in a course
begins the planning phase by asking, How?
If the answer is "by averaging at least 90 on the two major tests
and turning in four written reports,"
he can allocate the appropriate time periods to
study for the tests and prepare the reports.

Time organization or allocation alone is not adequate planning
(it answers the "when" but not the "how").
The parents with a goal of "teaching our four-year-old
the principle of obedience" cannot effectively plan
simply by allocating fifteen minutes a day to that goal.
They must develop a "how" plan
(through research and study and discussion together)
containing a method or approach designed to achieve their goal.
(*Then* they can determine and allocate the time required.)

(continued)

Consider the "how" plan of one mother:
"Being the mother of eight children, including four pre-schoolers,
has provided me with sufficient experience with frustration
to know that my emotional temperature rises rather rapidly,
especially when I'm tired. To remedy this,
I've found the following steps very practical:

1. Speaking softly to my children.
2. Sitting down with them at times when I feel
   I need to get my job done most,
   reading to them and expressing my love to them.
3. Reading the scriptures on a daily basis,
   preferably in the morning.
4. When I feel tension coming on,
   going to my room and praying, staying on my knees
   till I feel the calming influence.

S-20

Setting the sails is hard work.
In a two-master, the coordination of
the jib and mizzen with the mainsail
requires concentration
and the help of an experienced mate.

Planning is hard work.
Creative solutions or methods do not come easily.
They come through the laborious process of
focusing on the goal,
thinking about what is necessary to bring it about,
figuring out how to do what is necessary.

It often helps to plan together with someone —
a spouse on a family-goal-related plan,
a partner for a business goal, a counselor for one Church-related.

Environment is also a factor.
The further you can get from distractions,
the closer you can get to nature,
the better you can harness your powers of
concentration and creativity.

The planning must be done in connection
with each level of goal
but it is the weekly and monthly goals that lead directly
into the specific planning.
It is the planning phase that transforms monthly and weekly
goals from their written list
into the form of specific things to do and times to do them
and *onto* a calendar or date book
that you carry with you.

S-21

You might guess that a sailor who carefully plans
each day's course
would be less susceptible to the surprise and spontaneous delight
of each day's sailing.
Actually the contrary is true.
The captain who plots carefully his course
frees himself from
the worry and anxiety of moment-to-moment steering
and becomes better able to see and hear and smell
and appreciate
the sky and the waves.

G-21

At first impression, one might view
careful, regular goal-setting and planning
as the opposite
of living for the moment, in the present.
The fact is that one who has clear goals and plans
frees his mind from worry and anxiety
and becomes better able to enjoy the present.

The key is to move mentally into the future
during the Sunday planning sessions;
to make the decisions and chart the directions you can
for the week ahead and
then
to move back out of the future and into the present
and stay there (with the joy and the spontaneous moment
for the rest of the week).

Step 6
Trimming the Sails

In the process of sailing,
the wind changes, slightly, and the sail
starts to luff (to vibrate,
to slack, to lose the full force of the wind).
The sailor pulls in a sheet or adjusts a line;
the sail tightens and fills again to capacity
and the craft regains its speed.

The sea and the sky are never static;
they constantly change and move,
and the sail must, with each change,
be trimmed.

Step 6
Adjusting, Updating the Goals, Plans

In the process of life
we grow and change,
as does the world and the society around us,
and some of our goals and plans suddenly appear
too low or outdated
or somehow out of touch with the newer present.
Therefore, the goals and plans must be adjusted.
(Never to compromise or lower standards,
but to seize new-found opportunity or to raise sights
because of a newly discovered capacity, gift or ability.)

Neither we nor our world ever stands still.
Each constantly moves and changes.
Thus our intermediate goals and short-range plans must
correspondingly evolve and expand.

For example, I have observed many dedicated men
who have to make adjustments in their plans
because of Church callings which have come to them.
Fred Johnson's was a not untypical situation.

(continued)

Fred Johnson (not his real name)
was a successful sales manager.
Promotions had come to him
in the past year, and the fact that company officers
reminded him that he was being groomed for "better things"
caused him to consciously set his goals in that direction.
Then a call came to him
to serve as a mission president in the same country
where he had served as a missionary some twenty years before.
The call was accepted,
and within an amazingly short period of time
new goals and plans replaced
former goals and personal aspirations.

Two sailors, on a summer-long cruise through the
Caribbean's maze of islands,
adopted the practice of spending each weekend
in a small coastal port.
There they would talk to local sailors,
learn of the waters and islands ahead,
and adjust their pre-set course to conform to
what the residents told them
about the relative interest and safety of the alternative routes
for the coming week.

"Sunday session"
goal-setting and planning periods have already
been mentioned.
You can make them a "sail-trimming time"
by quickly reviewing all goals each week
(five-year, one-year, one-month)
before attempting to set the weekly plans.

Some weeks, as you review, all will "feel" right,
and you will be disposed to no changes.
Other weeks, though (due to some altered circumstance
or fresh opportunity or new insight into self),
you will see the clear chance to make a goal better
or to adjust a priority,
or to change an objective altogether.
Even more likely, you will see a new approach,
a better plan,
to reach an existing goal.
As you review each level of goals each week,
your subconscious mind will begin to do work on
the goals that you consciously know very little about.
The subconscious will become conscious as your
mind focuses on the goals each Sunday,
and you will find sharper, more refined approaches
than you could previously see.

S-24

The best sailing is filled with happy surprises —
a fresh breeze from an unexpected direction, or
a visible coral reef that has not been seen before.
A good sailor accepts new conditions as they come, and
turns them to his advantage;
he trims his sails constantly
to maximize the effect of the wind
and to stay always near his course.

The concept of "serendipity"
ties in well to the adjusting of goals, the trimming of sails.
Serendipity means:
"The ability, through sagacity and good fortune, to discover
something good while seeking something else."
Sagacity means acute sensitivity and awareness . . . the
kind of mental and spiritual alertness that allows one to
see
unexpected opportunities, unimagined new directions.

A person who is in tune with the Holy Ghost
can develop a kind of spiritual serendipity
that can serve as a guide in his life —
a guide for when and how to trim his sails.
Spiritual serendipity
is the attitude wherein one says, in essence:
"Heavenly Father, I have set goals in prayerful meditation
and I am pursuing those goals systematically.
However, my vision and knowledge of thy will are limited,
and I pray for thy guidance all along my path.
Help me to grow increasingly aware of thy will,
to see the things I should do as they come along,
to be ready to change any plan I have immediately
it becomes evident that there is another direction in which
thou wouldst have me go."

(continued)

G-24 *(continued)*

We can, through regular, evaluative Sunday sessions
and through spiritual serendipity,
adjust our goals and plans
to maximize our impact and to stay
always on the course the Lord has set before us.

Step 7
Wind

Regardless of the perfection
of the charted destination and
the set of the sails,
no sailboat can move without wind.

The wind is the force, the energy, the power
that propels the craft,
that takes it where it wants to go.

Step 7
Work

Regardless of the accuracy
of the objectives and
the creativity and brilliance of the plans,
nothing is accomplished without work.

Work and effort are the force, the power
that achieves the objectives
and fulfills the plans.

There is a four-letter, two-word phrase which has become
the motto of many great leaders
and which connotes the element most often neglected
by those who fail.
It reads:
"Do it."
The world is filled with dreamers of great dreams,
creators of great ideas,
formulators of great plans
whose lack of follow-through
prevents the dream from becoming a goal
and the goal from becoming a reality.

A sailboat moves best in a steady, moderate breeze.
Gusty, erratic winds may exert more total force
but they move the craft less total distance.

Goals are best achieved, and plans best fulfilled,
by well-timed, well-planned work, by
purposeful, *steady* effort.
When Joseph Smith said that
to work by faith is to work by mental effort and
not by physical force,
he was not downgrading hard labor;
he was merely teaching the fact that
careful prior thought produces
efficient, effective action.

How many times have you blindly tackled a job,
run into difficulty,
and been forced to step back, analyze the problem,
and take a more effective and purposeful approach?

Perhaps the single quality that separates the good sailor
from the average
is determination.
He reaches his destination each day;
he expects surprises and unexpected difficulty
(because the only predictable thing about the sea
is its unpredictability);
he meets the problems cheerfully, as they come,
and stays on his course.

Perhaps the greatest key of all is tenacity,
a stick-to-it quality, a bulldog toughness
that keeps a person with the task until it is done.

It is the work that gives credibility and confidence
to the goals and plans.
When a goal fails to be accomplished or a plan
goes unimplemented,
the next goal is set with less sense of reality,
the next plan with less purpose.
A pattern of slippage, a habit of procrastination,
and the goal-achievement principles are violated
and become dormant.
Sequential goals become impossible to reach,
and a general slippage of confidence
besets the goal-setter.

The person who has mastered the art and process
of goal achievement
expects unforeseen problems, relishes them,
turns them into opportunities, and always,
always
stays on course.

(continued)

When you think of turning problems into opportunities,
think on this example. A nineteen-year-old young man
had been planning and saving for a mission for
a good part of his life.
His parents unexpectedly suffered some financial reverses
and were not able to support him with funds.
He postponed his mission for one year
while he went to work and saved,
then he paid for his entire mission.
As a result, he was not only more self-reliant,
but he proved to be one of the more effective missionaries
because of his great desire to serve.

Postscript
Relationships over Achievements

A captain makes a grave mistake, if, in his mind,
"getting there"
becomes more important than the joy and relationships
of the journey.

In fact,
if he becomes so preoccupied with the destination
that he forgets and neglects his relationships
with his crew,
with the sea and the sky and the ocean around him,
with the boat itself,
he may never get there at all.

Postscript
Relationships over Achievements

This is one book in which the postscript
is at least as important
as the body of the book.
The postscript message is simply this:
If goal-setting and achievements occur at the *expense* of
relationships
it would be better for them not to occur at all.

Think of the old horse hitched to the plow.
On his head are the "blinders" that block his vision to
either side
so that he can see only the row ahead.
A person too preoccupied with the achievement of a goal
is like the horse,
blind to the beauty of the world around him,
blind to the needs and concerns of other people,
blind to the relationships that are eternal,
and seeing only the achievement that is temporary.

We are here to learn and to achieve —
but to do so in harmony
(not in conflict)
with our relationships with our brothers and sisters
and with our Heavenly Father.